U.S. ENVIRONMENTAL PROTECTION AGENCY

OFFICE OF INSPECTOR GENERAL

Office of Environmental Information Should Strengthen Controls Over Mobile Devices

Report No. 12-P-0427   April 25, 2012

Scan this mobile
code to learn more
about the EPA OIG.

Report Contributors: Patrick Gilbride
Erin Barnes-Weaver
Alicia Mariscal
Ashley Sellers-Hansen

Abbreviations

EDSD	Enterprise Desktop Solutions Division
EPA	U.S. Environmental Protection Agency
FY	Fiscal year
MD	Mobile device
OEI	Office of Environmental Information
OIG	Office of Inspector General
OTOP	Office of Technology Operations and Planning
SOP	Standard operating procedure
WCF	Working Capital Fund

U.S. Environmental Protection Agency
Office of Inspector General

12-P-0427
April 25, 2012

At a Glance

Why We Did This Review

The U.S. Environmental Protection Agency (EPA) Office of Inspector General (OIG) received a hotline complaint regarding misuse of mobile devices within the Office of Environmental Information (OEI). We reviewed the effectiveness of OEI's internal controls for mobile devices issued to OEI employees and contractors, focusing on issuance, disconnection, multiple devices, inappropriate use, and tracking and recovery.

Background

OEI provides technology services for EPA, including providing telecommunications and other technologies to support Agency activities. Executive Order 13589, issued on November 9, 2011, requires agencies to assess device usage and establish controls on unused or underutilized equipment or services, as well as limit the number of employee devices.

For further information, contact our Office of Congressional and Public Affairs at (202) 566-2391.

The full report is at:
www.epa.gov/oig/reports/2012/20120425-12-P-0427.pdf

Office of Environmental Information Should Strengthen Controls Over Mobile Devices

What We Found

Although OEI is in the process of developing policies for domestic and international mobile device usage, OEI has no organization-wide standard operating procedures that explain responsibilities for OEI employees and contractors regarding mobile devices. OEI currently does not have effective controls for the five areas of concern noted in the hotline complaint: issuance, disconnection, multiple devices, inappropriate use, and tracking and recovery.

We found that supervisors approve employee/contractor requests for mobile devices without guidance on determining the need for a device, and there is no guidance on the frequency with which employees can upgrade a device after it has been issued. OEI has also not established controls to determine when to disconnect devices; over a 6-month period in 2011, 68 OEI employees had zero usage of their mobile devices, incurring costs of about $29,360. Moreover, OEI managers tend not to be concerned about employees having multiple devices, and we found that eBusiness does not correctly reflect the number of devices issued to employees. Therefore, EPA may be paying for service on mobile devices that are not used. In addition, we found that one OEI employee and one OEI contractor made costly personal international phone calls. Finally, procedures and controls for tracking and recovering mobile devices are missing or ineffective.

What We Recommend

We recommend that OEI implement standard operating procedures for each step of the mobile device process to cover all aspects of issuance, disconnection, multiple devices, inappropriate use, and tracking and recovery. We also recommend that OEI follow up with OEI employees and contractors to determine business case justifications for users of multiple devices, and take appropriate action on unauthorized calls identified in the sample we reviewed. Lastly, we recommend that OEI finalize Agency-wide draft domestic and international mobile device procedures and develop other Agency-wide procedures as necessary. OEI concurred with the majority of our recommendations and described planned actions to address our recommendations. Our recommendations remain open pending OEI's corrective action plan with milestone dates, as well as additional specificity from OEI on monitoring inappropriate device usage.

UNITED STATES ENVIRONMENTAL PROTECTION AGENCY
WASHINGTON, D.C. 20460

April 25, 2012

MEMORANDUM

SUBJECT: Office of Environmental Information Should Strengthen Controls
Over Mobile Devices
Report No. 12-P-0427

FROM: Arthur A. Elkins, Jr.

TO: Malcolm D. Jackson
Assistant Administrator for Environmental Information and
Chief Information Officer

This is our report on the subject audit conducted by the Office of Inspector General (OIG) of the U.S. Environmental Protection Agency (EPA). This report contains findings that describe the problems the OIG has identified and corrective actions the OIG recommends. This report represents the opinion of the OIG and does not necessarily represent the final EPA position. Final determinations on matters in this report will be made by EPA managers in accordance with established audit resolution procedures.

Action Required

In accordance with EPA Manual 2750, you are required to provide a written response to this report within 90 calendar days. You should include a corrective actions plan for agreed-upon actions, including milestone dates. We will post your response on the OIG's public website, along with our memorandum commenting on your response. Please provide your response as an Adobe PDF file that complies with the accessibility requirements of Section 508 of the Rehabilitation Act of 1973, as amended. The final response should not contain data that you do not want released to the public; if your response contains such data, you should identify the data for redaction or removal. We have no objections to the further release of this report to the public. We will post this report to our website at http://www.epa.gov/oig.

If you or your staff have any questions regarding this report, please contact Melissa Heist at (202) 566-0899 or heist.melissa@epa.gov, or Patrick Gilbride at (303) 312-6969 or gilbride.patrick@epa.gov.

Table of Contents

Chapters

Appendices

Chapter 1
Introduction

Purpose

The U.S. Environmental Protection Agency (EPA) Office of Inspector General (OIG) received a hotline complaint on May 16, 2011, regarding misuse of mobile device (MD)[1] services within the Office of Environmental Information (OEI). The complaint alleged five areas of concern: issuance, disconnection, employee usage of multiple MDs, fraudulent use, and tracking and recovery. Accordingly, our objective was to determine whether OEI has internal controls for OEI employee and contractor MDs, and whether they effectively control:

- Issuance
- Disconnection
- Use of multiple devices
- Inappropriate use
- Processes for tracking and recovery

Background

Internal Control Standards

The U.S. Government Accountability Office *Standards for Internal Control in the Federal Government* defines "internal control" as an integral component of an organization's management that provides reasonable assurance of effective and efficient operations and compliance with applicable laws and regulations. Office of Management and Budget Circular A-123 (revised 2004) states, among other matters, that agency managers should take timely and effective action to correct internal control deficiencies. As the Government Accountability Office recognized, an internal control comprises the plans, methods, and procedures used to meet missions, goals, and objectives and, in doing so, supports performance-based management. Internal control is not one event, but a series of actions and activities that occur throughout an entity's operations and on an ongoing basis.

Office of Environmental Information

Headed by the Chief Information Officer, OEI supports the Agency's mission to protect public health and the environment by providing environmental information that can be used to inform decisions, improve management, document

---

[1] For the purposes of this report, we define MDs as cellular phones and pocket-sized computing devices, typically having a display screen with touch input or a miniature keyboard (e.g., BlackBerry).

performance, and measure success. OEI manages the life cycle of information to support EPA's mission. According to its website, OEI:

- Identifies and implements information technology and information management solutions
- Ensures the quality of EPA's information and the efficiency and reliability of EPA's technology, data collection, exchange efforts, and access services
- Provides technology services and manages EPA's information technology investments

OEI also works with many internal and external stakeholders and partners to implement information-related policies and procedures. OEI had approximately 416 employees as of June 2011. In fiscal year (FY) 2011, OEI spent $465,871 on MD services.

OEI's Office of Technology Operations and Planning (OTOP) supports the Agency's information systems and products. OTOP's Enterprise Desktop Solutions Division (EDSD) provides local area network, telecommunications, call center, and desktop support, and manages MD service.

Working Capital Fund and eBusiness

OEI OTOP procures mobile telecommunication services through EPA's Working Capital Fund (WCF). EPA's WCF operates like a commercial business, offering a wide range of administrative services, including financial management, information technology, telecommunications, rent and facilities, printing, and transportation services. EPA's WCF provides services in four business lines, one of which includes the Agency's computer and telecommunications services. All EPA WCF business is conducted through eBusiness, a Web application in which users establish the necessary accounts, shop for WCF products and services via an online catalog, obtain products and services, and monitor usage. EPA's application of the WCF and utilization of eBusiness promotes transparency by making product, cost, and usage information available in a Web-based platform accessible to EPA office account managers and supervisors.

Policies and Procedures for Mobile Devices

Limited Personal Use of Government Office Equipment

In 2004, EPA issued Order 2101.0, *Limited Personal Use of Government Office Equipment*, which applies to all employees. The policy states that employees may use government office equipment only for authorized purposes. The policy also authorizes limited personal use during non-work time if the personal use:

- Involves minimal additional expense to the government
- Does not reduce productivity or interfere with official duties or the official duties of others
- Is by an employee already authorized to use the equipment for official government business
- Is legal and appropriate

The policy specifies that users should not expect privacy when engaged in limited personal use of government office equipment, and that users should not give the appearance that personal use is in an official capacity. The policy also gives examples of inappropriate personal uses (e.g., making long-distance phone calls), and the consequences for misuse of government office equipment. The policy explains that managers and supervisors may further restrict personal use based on the needs of the office or problems with unauthorized or inappropriate use.

Cellular Equipment/Services Acquisition and Use Manual

Issued in 2002, EPA's *Cellular Equipment/Services Acquisition and Use Manual* establishes directives for the acquisition and use of cellular equipment and services nationwide. The manual states:

> Cellular telephones and other cellular equipment are to be used only for the conduct of official Government business. Federal Information Resources Management Regulation (FIRMR) and Code of Federal Regulations, Titles 5 and 41, address disciplinary actions and collection efforts that can be taken against Federal employees who misuse Government property or services. This includes the unauthorized use of Government owned property, such as cellular devices, with the intent to later reimburse the Government.

The manual requires cellular instruments to be accounted for and managed in accordance with appropriate EPA property accountability procedures.

Personal Property Management Policies

EPA's *Personal Property Policy and Procedures Manual* is the authoritative reference for EPA's management of personal property. The manual provides policy and procedural guidance on personal property management issues for EPA employees and contractors. The manual defines personal property as any property except real property (and defines real property as land, together with the improvements, structures, and fixtures located thereon). All EPA employees and contractors must adhere to the policy and procedures set forth in the manual when executing personal property management functions on behalf of EPA.

Custodial Officer Online Training and Guide

EPA's Custodial Officer Online Training explains a custodial officer's responsibilities for the three stages in the personal property life cycle—acquisition, utilization, and disposition. The training describes a number of standard operating procedures (SOPs) (e.g., conducting annual and quarterly physical inventories and records management), some of which serve as internal controls. The *Custodial Officers' Guide* is an extension of the online training, with more detailed examples. This guide provides information on rules and regulations that form the basis for property management, discusses the property management program within EPA, and focuses on the specific roles and responsibilities of a custodial officer within the property management structure. As with the training, the guide offers examples of SOPs and internal controls (e.g., key forms and documents for different tasks, a physical inventory process map, and a custodial officer checklist).

Noteworthy Achievements

EPA's Mobile Device Service Review and Optimization Analysis

In August 2010, EPA hired a contractor to execute a service review for the Agency's MD service program, including benchmarking current MD service plans and support contracts, documenting total cost of ownership, and recommending service optimization opportunities. As part of this study, the contractor reviewed usage data as a percentage of total available plan minutes to identify devices that were not being used or were underused over a 6-month period (January–March 2010 and May–July 2010). MD usage was categorized as falling under 1, 10, 20, and 30 percent of the monthly plan available minute allotment. Although the contractor found that, overall, the MD service program is sound, the report identified areas where EPA should take immediate action to further optimize the quality of the service and reduce costs associated with service delivery.

Recent Procedural Document and SOP Drafts

In 2011, OEI drafted a number of procedural documents and SOPs pertaining to MDs specifically or personal property in general. These include:

- *International Travel Procedure for Mobile Devices*, which covers the process EPA employees and contractors must follow to comply with the provisions of the Agency's network security policy and safeguard EPA-issued MDs while on international travel

- *Mobile Device and Wireless Network Procedures*, which includes requirements for implementing and managing the domestic use of EPA-owned MDs, including only using MDs to perform official government duties
- An Asset Management Plan for the proper management of all information technology assets, including SOPs to address acquisition, use, and physical security
- *OEI Personal Property Management*, which provides OEI employees with the SOPs to properly acquire, receive, inventory, maintain, and reutilize or dispose of personal property.

Though not in place during the time of our review, once finalized, these policies and SOPs could help address the problems we describe in chapter 2.

Use of Pooled Voice Plans

To anticipate and mitigate overages by any one user, EPA uses a 200-minute pooled plan with one vendor and a 300-minute pooled plan with another. The pooled plans makes these minutes available to anyone on the account, which can help the Agency avoid costs for overages. EPA has never exceeded the total minute allowance of each pooled plan, and uses roughly 85 percent of the minutes available in carrier pools each month.

Scope and Methodology

We conducted our field work from June 2011 to February 2012 in accordance with generally accepted government auditing standards. Those standards require that we plan and perform our review to obtain sufficient, appropriate evidence to provide a reasonable basis for our findings and conclusions based on our objective. We believe that the evidence obtained provides a reasonable basis for our findings and conclusions based on our objective.

To address our objective, we reviewed policies and procedures (OEI-specific and Agency-wide) for MDs as well as those related to the personal use of MDs, including those described in the "Background" section. We also reviewed Executive Order 13589, *Promoting Efficient Spending*, issued on November 9, 2011, which asks each federal agency to take steps to limit the number of MDs issued to employees.

We interviewed the OIG budget team (in charge of MD payments) to benchmark and understand the process for managing MDs prior to discussions with OEI. We then interviewed OEI headquarters staff responsible for developing and overseeing policies and procedures, including:

- WCF MD services manager
- Associate director for business management

- Acting branch chief, Call Center and Business Management Branch
- Account managers
- WCF coordinator
- Property/custodial officers

We also interviewed a regional technical services unit chief to get an "outside OEI" perspective on some of the allegations raised in the hotline complaint, specifically on multiple MDs and inappropriate use. We also corresponded with the hotline complainant and reviewed materials the complainant provided. Specific steps we took to address each of the five areas of concern in the hotline complaint are presented in appendix A.

Limitations

We were unable to determine the total number of MDs issued to OEI contractors through the WCF. OEI does not know whether its employees or contractors received MDs through other OEI contracts outside of OEI's EDSD Service Agreement in eBusiness. In addition, EDSD did not know of a way to obtain that information. We were also unable to determine how much OEI spends on MD accessories each year because OEI does not track the cost of MD accessories or the accessories themselves.

Chapter 2
OEI Lacks Effective Internal Controls and Policies for Mobile Devices

OEI supervisors issue MDs without guidance, and no clear requirements exist for how long employees should keep MDs before upgrading devices. Also:

- A number of OEI employees do not use their MDs.
- OEI managers have little concern about employees having multiple MDs.
- One OEI employee and contractor used their EPA-issued MDs to make personal international calls.
- The Agency does not track MD accessory purchases
- eBusiness does not correctly reflect the number of MDs issued to employees.

A number of Agency-wide policies and procedures relate to the use of MDs, and OEI is in the process of developing policies on domestic and international MD usage. However, OEI does not currently have effective internal controls or SOPs for OEI employees and contractors addressing MD issuance, disconnection, employees with multiple MDs, inappropriate use of MDs, and MD tracking and recovery. As a result, EPA may be wasting government resources by allowing some OEI employees to have multiple MDs without sufficient justification, allowing employees to have MDs without a sufficient business case, and incurring high charges from employees and contractors who make personal international calls.

Internal Controls and Policies for Mobile Devices Are Not Effective

Initial Mobile Device Issuance and Upgrades

Our findings indicate that a majority of OEI staff have an MD, but some may not need the device to perform their official government duties. Further, employees are upgrading their MDs more frequently than the industry standard. Executive Order 13589, *Promote Efficient Spending*, asks each federal agency to take steps to limit the number of MDs issued to employees. We found that OEI lacks SOPs regarding MD issuance and upgrades for OEI employees and contractors. As a result, EPA may be wasting resources by issuing MDs to employees who do not need them and upgrading MDs earlier than necessary.

OEI does not have guidance for managers to help them determine whether a business case exists for an employee to be issued an MD. OEI has issued 434 MDs—306 to OEI employees and 128 to OEI contractors. As of June 2011, OEI had approximately 416 employees, and was unable to provide information on the number of contractor employees. When OEI employees need an MD, they place the request with their immediate supervisor. Currently, neither OEI nor an OEI-contracted firm require that supervisors apply criteria or complete any form on the business case justification for MD requests, which results in OEI supervisors making MD approvals without guidance. In FY 2011, OEI spent $465,871 on MD service.

OEI does not have a policy on how frequently OEI employees and contractors can upgrade their MDs. According to OEI, cell phone carriers require federal employees to wait a minimum of 1 year before they can request an upgraded device. We learned that, in some cases, OEI employees upgrade their devices before 1 year by canceling their current line and transferring their device to someone else in OEI. Two custodial officers thought that OEI staff should be required to keep a device for 1 year before requesting an upgrade. A regional technical services unit chief believes it is reasonable to get a new device every 2 years.

We also found that no policies or SOPs exist for custodial officers regarding the appropriateness of type and number of MD accessories. OEI bankcard holders or custodial officers purchase MD accessories through eBusiness and the WCF, or with a bankcard. MD accessories, including cases, headsets, and chargers, can be purchased with a bankcard because they are nonaccountable property, do not contain any EPA data, and do not need an EPA property decal. OEI does not track the cost of MD accessories or the accessories themselves. One account manager said that the accessories may not be utilized.

OEI has drafted the *Mobile Device and Wireless Network Procedures*, which aims to require employees and contractors to submit requests to receive an MD, along with a business justification, to their manager for consideration. However, OEI has not finalized these procedures.

Mobile Device Disconnection

OEI does not direct custodial officers or account managers to regularly request and review utilization reports, which are available at any time, and OEI staff persons working with property are not always notified when an employee leaves EPA or transfers to a new EPA program office. Executive Order 13589, *Promoting Efficient Spending*, states that agencies should assess current device usage and establish controls to ensure that agencies do not pay for underutilized or unused equipment or services. However, no SOPs exist regarding disconnection for OEI employees and contractors, nor are there controls for supervisory review/renewal of the need for continued MD service. As a result, EPA may be paying for MD service on devices that are not being used.

A November 2011 zero usage report[2] found that 68 OEI employees had zero usage over a 6-month period in 2011. The cost for these 68 monthly MD service

---

[2] A zero usage report identifies employees who did not use their cell phones or BlackBerrys in any manner.

bills for the 6-month period was approximately $29,360.[3] OEI indicated that these zero usage users may need to retain active service on these accounts because, depending on the employee, the lack of use may be cyclical or the MD may only be needed for travel or emergency situations.

In addition, OEI staff responsible for property (hereafter "OEI property staff") are not always notified when an employee leaves EPA or transfers to a new EPA program office. The eBusiness FY 2011 MD Service Description states that the customer must cancel MD service through eBusiness. However, an OEI property staff person indicated that OEI employees are unsure of the procedures to follow when they no longer need an MD, move to a different EPA program office, or leave the Agency. Thus, OEI property staff are not notified when a user's service should be disconnected. One OEI property staff person contacts MD numbers if questions exist regarding usage and whether the employee still works for OEI. This OEI property staff person stated that the MD is disconnected if repeated messages go unanswered or if call recipients do not identify themselves as EPA employees.

Multiple Mobile Devices

OEI allows some employees to have both a cell phone and a BlackBerry for comfort purposes (i.e., employees claim to be more comfortable using a cellular phone to make calls and a Blackberry to check e-mail), and account managers and custodial officers are not updated with the correct end user information, resulting in inaccurate data in eBusiness. Executive Order 13589, *Promote Efficient Spending,* asks each federal agency to take steps to limit the number of MDs issued to employees. OEI lacks internal controls regarding multiple devices; it has no SOPs that prohibit employees from having multiple MDs. Further, inaccurate information in eBusiness may falsely indicate that staff have multiple MDs. As a result, EPA is unnecessarily expending resources on multiple MDs for OEI employees, and may be paying for MD service on devices that are not being used.

eBusiness records from June 14, 2011, indicate that 49 OEI employees had multiple devices. On October 19, 2011, we requested that OEI employees with more than one MD provide confirmation of use for each registered device as well as a business case justification for using more than one MD. Of the 44 responses from the 49 OEI employees we contacted,[4] 27 confirmed that they only have one device, which means that eBusiness does not have accurate information. Those with multiple MDs gave varied responses as to why they need those devices. Table 1 lists employee and manager justifications for multiple MDs.

---

[3] Calculated by multiplying the average per-user monthly bill of $71.96 for OEI MD service by 68 (number of employees) and 6 (number of months), rounding up to the nearest dollar.

[4] We learned that five of those we contacted are no longer employed by OEI, and the status of their devices is unknown.

Table 1: OEI justifications for employee possession of multiple MDs

➤ Registering extra devices for future use by new employees	➤ Ensuring communications during international travel
➤ Needing a working device when original is broken	➤ Being able to provide a device if a senior manager/official requests one
➤ Neglecting to return an international loaner device	➤ Needing an employee to be available around the clock
➤ Needing a back-up device for work-related travel	➤ Providing a device to a contractor

Source: OIG analysis of responses provided by OEI staff and MD service manager.

While we found little concern among OEI managers about employees having multiple MDs, OEI property staff responsible for tracking inventory expressed concern about this issue. One custodial officer indicated that some OEI property staff will review inventory on a monthly basis to ensure that eBusiness has MDs correctly registered to the proper end user. Multiple MDs often appear in eBusiness under one person's name, but the MD does not actually belong to that person. Because account managers and custodial officers are not updated with the correct end user information, eBusiness does not reflect accurate information. OEI recognizes that outdated information in eBusiness can indicate that some staff have multiple MDs when they may not.

Inappropriate Use of Mobile Devices

We found that one OEI employee and one OEI contractor incurred high international roaming charges on their EPA-issued MDs while traveling for personal reasons. EPA Order 2101.0, *Limited Personal Use of Government Office Equipment*, states that employees may use government office equipment only for authorized purposes. OEI has not established internal controls for inappropriate use of MDs. At the time of our review, there were no finalized SOPs defining inappropriate use of MDs or the manner in which confirmed cases of inappropriate use should be handled. When inappropriate use goes unnoticed, EPA pays for excess charges.

We reviewed call detail reports[5] and eBusiness/WCF billing reports covering a 6-month period (January–June 2011)[6] to identify questionable costs, including high costs and international charges. We found that 19 OEI employees and contractors had made personal international phone calls during that 6-month period, incurring high charges as a result. Phone calls were made to/from, among other places, Denmark, El Salvador, Ethiopia, France, Germany, Honduras, Italy, Kenya, Spain, Sudan, and Turkey. International charges for these 19 employees

---

[5] Call detail reports provide detailed information regarding all incoming and outgoing phone calls made to and from an MD. For our review, OEI provided call detail reports from four cell phone carriers—AT&T, Verizon, Sprint, and T-Mobile.

[6] The OEI billing invoices we reviewed follow a billing cycle that begins the last week of one month and ends the last week of the following month. Therefore, some of the charges included in our analysis occurred either in December 2010 or July 2011. Two examples of billing invoice statements that included these months are those from 12/24/10 to 01/23/11 and 06/24/11 to 07/23/11.

and contractors during the 6 months totaled $4,136.49. OEI management stated that unless an OEI employee is attending a conference in an international location, the majority of OEI's work happens domestically. This statement suggests that most international calls are not taking place for business purposes.

From the sample of 27 employees and contractors, we selected for further review 1 OEI employee and 1 OEI contractor who had inappropriately used their MDs while traveling internationally for personal reasons.[7] Managers confirmed that both individuals traveled abroad for personal reasons and used their government-issued MDs to make personal phone calls and send text messages while traveling. The OEI employee incurred charges of $1,331.37 for international roaming and other usage charges in a 1-month period. The contractor incurred charges of $824.69 for international roaming and other usage charges over a 2-month period. For both individuals, the charges went unnoticed by account managers and supervisors, and EPA paid for the charges.

OEI supervisors and account managers do not review or monitor invoices in eBusiness on a regular basis, but rather at the end of the fiscal year, and one account manager is responsible for reviewing the records of hundreds of employees/contractors. However, if inappropriate use becomes apparent, supervisors deal with it on a case-by-case basis. Some supervisors may terminate MD service or expect the employee to repay the costs. In our sample, the OEI employee received a warning, whereas the contractor's supervisor was going to direct the contractor to repay the costs of the personal international calls.

OEI has two draft procedural documents related to inappropriate use of MDs. The draft *Mobile Device and Wireless Network Procedures* instructs EPA employees, managers, contractors, and grantees to consult with their managers if they have questions regarding the appropriate use of their MDs. The draft *International Travel Procedure for Mobile Devices* states that EPA-issued MDs and laptops are only for government-authorized uses.

Processes for Tracking and Recovering Mobile Devices

OEI does not effectively track and recover all MDs. The *Custodial Officers' Guide* states that custodial officers are to enter property data into receiving logs and apply decals to the property, enter the information into the Integrated Financial Management System,[8] and deliver the decaled property to the end user. The guide and the Office of Administration and Resources Management Facilities Management and Services Division's *EPA Personal Property Policy and Procedures Manual* lists cellular telephones and BlackBerrys as sensitive items. Both define sensitive items as nonexpendable items that may be converted to

---

[7] Our billing invoice analysis found that 8 of 27 OEI employees and contractors did not make any international calls. We selected 1 OEI employee and 1 OEI contractor for further review. Of the 27 in our sample, we did not verify whether the remaining 17 employees and contractors with international calls made those calls for personal reasons.
[8] As of October 21, 2011, Compass replaced the Integrated Financial Management System.

private use or have a high potential for theft, and that must be recorded as accountable property. This type of accountability requires property to be tracked throughout its life cycle, regardless of cost or value. However, OEI employees and contractors do not have SOPs on their role in the MD tracking and recovery process, resulting in inaccurate equipment records and wasted resources in trying to reconcile and track property.

We verified that OEI custodial officers decal MDs as sensitive items, maintain property inventory spreadsheets, and report lost or stolen MDs to the Board of Survey.[9] However, we found that (1) OEI employees and contractors do not always notify custodial officers when MDs are transferred to other end users; (2) on some occasions, when a new employee needs a device, OEI will put a current employee's name on the account but will not go back into eBusiness to update records to reflect the correct end user; and (3) OEI employees are unaware of what to do with MDs once they no longer need them and do not properly return MDs when they are no longer in use. As a result of these situations, MDs may not be registered to the correct end user in eBusiness.

Conclusion

Developing and implementing organization-wide, detailed SOPs will help ensure that OEI has controls for issuance, disconnection, multiple MDs, inappropriate use, and tracking and recovery. Further, it is important that OEI improve its financial management of MDs by requiring business case justifications for users generally and users of multiple MDs, and taking appropriate action to identify and eliminate unauthorized calls.

Recommendations

We recommend that the Assistant Administrator for Environmental Information and Chief Information Officer:

1. Develop and implement SOPs for OEI employees and contractors, as well as account managers/property staff, on each step of the MD process. SOPs should:

   a. Require custodial officers to, on a quarterly basis, verify/confirm the accuracy of eBusiness information on MD user registration and utilization.

   b. Develop standardized business case justifications for issuing an MD that supervisors can utilize. Require supervisors to review justifications annually.

---

[9] The Board of Survey serves as a fact-finding body charged with determining the circumstances and conditions of each case in which EPA property is declared lost, damaged, or destroyed.

c. Develop an appropriate MD upgrade and replacement schedule consistent with the industry standard for upgrading wireless devices that includes conditions and justifications for approving upgrades sooner than the standard.

d. Address the number and type of MD accessories that may be purchased, and require custodial officers to track accessory costs.

e. Include standard procedures for addressing inappropriate use of an MD, including consequences.

f. Develop eBusiness design changes that would trigger the system to notify account managers when a predetermined cost threshold is reached, which may indicate potentially inappropriate use of an MD.

g. Allow approved users to possess either a cell phone or a BlackBerry, or require additional documented justification and annual review if an employee requires multiple devices.

h. Review the business need for MD users with low utilization of their monthly plan minute allotments (less than 1, 10, 20, and 30 percent utilization as described in EPA's Mobile Device Service Review and Optimization Analysis) and terminate service where appropriate.

i. Require end users to notify their property staff when they no longer need a device, transfer to another EPA program office, or leave the Agency. Instruct end users on the proper procedure for turning in their MDs.

2. Follow up with OEI managers and determine:

a. Whether there is a valid business case justification for those staff using multiple MDs, and determine whether one of the devices should be returned to the Agency.

b. Whether the international calls made during January–June 2011 by the remaining 17 OEI employees and contractors we identified in our sample of 27 were inappropriate, and take action based on SOPs developed per recommendation 1.

3. Finalize Agency-wide draft domestic and international MD procedures and develop other Agency-wide procedures as necessary that consider SOPs that encompass the areas listed in recommendation 1.

Agency Comments and OIG Evaluation

OEI concurred with all of our recommendations except for 1-d and 1-f. On 1-d, OEI correctly notes that EPA's *Personal Property Policy and Procedures Manual* does not include items valued at less than $5,000 unless they are sensitive items; however, the Custodial Officers' Guide does require an EPA property decal on accessories. We support OEI's plan to include in the SOP a standardized accessories list in the business case justifications for MD issuance, and we urge OEI to base accessory purchases on need and requests from users. This would mitigate one instance we heard about during our review where an account manager said they ordered all accessories that came with the device in advance and then gave them to the employee who said they did not want them. The account manager said they kept unwanted accessories and gave them to another person at a later time, and learned not to order as many accessories before users request them. Another account manager said that accessories are usually approved for staff, and OEI does not know how much it spends on accessories each year. We agree that OEI's planned SOP should address necessity and use of MD accessories.

On 1-f, we agree with OEI that adequate information sources exist where account managers can monitor mobile device usage; however, we learned that account managers do not regularly review these sources. One account manager, who oversees hundreds of contractors, said they only review usage once a year at the end of the fiscal year and not on a more routine basis. This account manager oversaw the inappropriate charges that formed the basis for the May 2011 hotline complaint to our office; however, the account manager did not notice these charges until the manager's review at the end of the fiscal year (September 2011). As of the date of an interview with us in October 2011, another account manager had not reviewed any usage in 2011, and this account manager only oversees 12 users as opposed to the aforementioned account manager's workload. While OEI receives "zero usage reports" from carriers on a regular basis and custodial officers and account managers can request a utilization report at any time, account managers do not routinely review them but for once annually. As such, OEI needs to do more than "educate" account managers on usage reports. This recommendation remains unresolved pending more specificity from OEI on monitoring inappropriate device usage. OEI's comments on not exceeding Agency-wide pooled minutes does not address the appropriateness of having staff retain devices when those staff had zero usage over a 6-month time frame.

Appendix B contains OEI's full response to our draft report and planned actions to address our recommendations. Our recommendations remain open pending OEI's corrective action plan with milestone dates—particularly for the primary SOP OEI cites throughout its response—as well as additional specificity from OEI on monitoring inappropriate device usage.

Status of Recommendations and Potential Monetary Benefits

		RECOMMENDATIONS				POTENTIAL MONETARY BENEFITS (in $000s)	
Rec. No.	Page No.	Subject	Status[1]	Action Official	Planned Completion Date	Claimed Amount	Agreed-To Amount
1	12	Develop and implement SOPs for OEI employees and contractors, as well as account managers/ property staff, on each step of the MD process. SOPs should:		Assistant Administrator for Environmental Information and Chief Information Officer			
		a. Require custodial officers to, on a quarterly basis, verify/confirm the accuracy of eBusiness information on MD user registration and utilization.	O				
		b. Develop standardized business case justifications for issuing an MD that supervisors can utilize. Require supervisors to review justifications annually.	O				
		c. Develop an appropriate MD upgrade and replacement schedule consistent with the industry standard for upgrading wireless devices that includes conditions and justifications for approving upgrades sooner than the standard.	O				
		d. Address the number and type of MD accessories that may be purchased, and require custodial officers to track accessory costs.	O				
		e. Include standard procedures for addressing inappropriate use of an MD, including consequences.	O				
		f. Develop eBusiness design changes that would trigger the system to notify account managers when a predetermined cost threshold is reached, which may indicate potentially inappropriate use of an MD.	O				
		g. Allow approved users to possess either a cell phone or a BlackBerry, or require additional documented justification and annual review if an employee requires multiple devices.	O				
		h. Review the business need for MD users with low utilization of their monthly plan minute allotments (less than 1, 10, 20, or 30 percent utilization as described in EPA's Mobile Device Service Review and Optimization Analysis) and terminate service where appropriate.	O			$29	
		i. Require end users to notify their property staff when they no longer need a device, transfer to another EPA program office, or leave the Agency. Instruct end users on the proper procedure for turning in their MDs.	O				

Rec. No.	Page No.	Subject	Status[1]	Action Official	Planned Completion Date	Claimed Amount	Agreed-To Amount
2	13	Follow up with OEI managers and determine:		Assistant Administrator for Environmental Information and Chief Information Officer			
		a. Whether there is a valid business case justification for those staff using multiple MDs, and determine whether one of the devices should be returned to the Agency.	O				
		b. Whether the international calls made during January–June 2011 by the remaining 17 OEI employees and contractors we identified in our sample of 27 were inappropriate, and take action based on SOPs developed per recommendation 1.	O				
3	13	Finalize Agency-wide draft domestic and international MD procedures and develop other Agency-wide procedures as necessary that consider SOPs that encompass the areas listed in recommendation 1.	O	Assistant Administrator for Environmental Information and Chief Information Officer			

[1] O = recommendation is open with agreed-to corrective actions pending
C = recommendation is closed with all agreed-to actions completed
U = recommendation is unresolved with resolution efforts in progress

Details on Scope and Methodology

Table A-1: OIG steps to investigate hotline complaint

Area of concern	Steps
Issuance	➢ Reviewed eBusiness records and other sources to identify the number of OEI staff with MDs and related costs ➢ Discussed business case justifications with supervisors
Disconnection	➢ Interviewed a custodial officer on the process for assessing usage and determining disconnections ➢ Reviewed a November 2011 zero usage report to identify OEI employees who did not use their MDs in any manner over a 6-month period
Multiple MDs	➢ Reviewed eBusiness records and files OEI provided identifying staff with multiple MDs ➢ Queried staff, managers, and a custodial officer as to the business case justification for having multiple MDs

Inappropriate use	➢ Reviewed call detail reports and eBusiness/WCF billing reports covering a 6-month period (January–June 2011) to identify questionable costs, including high costs and international charges
	   ○ Held a webinar with the WCF Mobile Device Services Manager and an EDSD contractor to understand how the source data delivered from the carriers is converted into a Microsoft Excel file, known as a CDR, which OEI provided us for our analysis.
	   ○ Using a filter in the CDRs, we identified all calls made to international locations and calls with charges over $20.00.
	   ○ We analyzed the eBusiness/WCF billing reports by the OEI account managers, which resulted from our CDR analysis, for international roaming charges and charges over $100.00.
	➢ Reviewed billing invoices on a sample of OEI and contractor personnel we identified as having questionable charges and discussed charges and responsive actions with account managers and two supervisors (one who supervises an EPA employee and one who supervises a contractor)
	   ○ Held a webinar with a Business Analyst/Billing Invoices Manager and the WCF Mobile Device Services Manager to understand how OEI downloaded the MD billing invoices from the carrier website to provide them to us in an Adobe PDF format for our analysis.
	   ○ The final billing invoices sample included all persons identified with international roaming charges in the CDR and eBusiness billing reports by account manager.

Tracking and recovery	➢ Reviewed eBusiness records to ascertain appropriate end user registrations ➢ Interviewed custodial officers on the process for obtaining MDs once staff no longer needs them ➢ Reviewed a memo titled "Missing Accountable Personal Property" to determine if missing items of accountable property were MDs within OEI

Source: OIG.

Office of Environmental Information's
Response to Draft Report

UNITED STATES ENVIRONMENTAL PROTECTION AGENCY
WASHINGTON, D.C. 20460

MAR 2 6 2012

OFFICE OF
ENVIRONMENTAL INFORMATION

MEMORANDUM

SUBJECT: OEI Response to the OIG's Draft Audit Report, "Office of Environmental
Information Should Strengthen Controls Over Mobile Devices, Project Number
OA-FY11-0278"

FROM: Malcolm D. Jackson
Assistant Administrator and Chief Information Officer

TO: Arthur Elkins
Inspector General

In response to the draft Audit Report, *"Office of Environmental Information Should Strengthen Controls
Over Mobile Devices, Project Number OA-FYII-0278"*, the Office of Environmental Information is
pleased to provide you with our responses to the following OIG recommendations.

1. Develop and implement Standard Operating Procedures (SOPs) for OEI employees and contractors, as
   well as account managers/property staff, on each step of the Mobile Devices (MD) process. SOPs should:

a. Require custodial officers to, on a quarterly basis, verify/confirm the accuracy of eBusiness information
   on MD user registration and utilization.

   *Concur. OEI's Office of Planning, Resources and Outreach (OPRO) plans to develop a SOP to ensure
   that both the custodial officers and Working Capital Fund (WCF) Account Managers do their part to
   verify/confirm the accuracy of eBusiness registration and utilization.*

b. Develop standardized business case justifications for issuing a MD that supervisors can utilize. Require
   supervisors to review justifications annually.

   *Concur. The planned SOP will develop standardized business case justifications for issuing a MD that a
   supervisor can utilize. OEI plans to develop the SOP to require supervisors to review justifications
   annually by coordinating with the WCF account manager.*

c. Develop an appropriate MD upgrade and replacement schedule consistent with the industry standard for upgrading wireless devices that includes conditions and justifications for approving upgrades sooner than the standard.

Concur. OEI plans to develop two actions for this recommendation. The two actions are as follows:

1. *Develop an appropriate MD upgrade and replacement schedule consistent with the industry standard for upgrading wireless devices.*
2. *Promulgate a schedule that includes conditions and justifications for approving upgrades sooner than the standard.*

In response to action 1: OTOP procures mobile devices for EPA WCF customers (including OEI) who place orders in eBusiness using EPA contracts with our carriers that were established via Blanket Purchase Agreements (BPAs). In turn, these BPAs use GSA's Federal Supply Schedule (FSS) contracts with our carriers that have terms/conditions that dictate when a mobile device can be upgraded which is based on the length of time each line of service has been in place. Per GSA FSS contracts with the carriers, the minimum length of time for an existing line of service that qualifies for a zero cost equipment upgrade is one year. These terms/conditions apply across all agencies that use GSA's FSS carrier contracts including EPA. These one-year terms/conditions are applicable to the federal government which is different than the commercial service entity carriers provided to consumers (typically 18 months to 2-years before an upgrade can be requested).

EPA WCF customers can select either zero cost equipment or equipment that has a significant government discount that is offered by the carrier that is much lower. Most EPA WCF customers, including OEI customers, select the zero cost equipment option available from the carriers.

Corrective Action:
OTOP will recommend/communicate via established communication sources (i.e., WCF monthly reports, etc.) that WCF customers should use the zero cost equipment option when replacing mobile devices. The aforementioned action will be communicated to OEIIOPRO within a 30-day time frame commencing in April 2012. In addition, OTOP will provide this same information for inclusion in the Agency Mobile Device and Wireless procedure when finalized.

In response to action 2: OPRO plans to include in the SOP a schedule that includes conditions and justifications for approving upgrades sooner than the standard.

d. Address the number and type of MD accessories that may be purchased, and require custodial officers to track accessory costs.

Do not concur. OEI believes it is not efficient or in keeping with Agency policy for custodial officers to track MD accessories. In addition, tracking the cost of such items alone is not likely to decrease acquisitions of MD accessories. EPA's Personal Property Policy and Procedures manual does not include items valued at less than $5,000 unless they are sensitive items.

However, OEI plans to include in the SOP a standard accessories list in the standardized business case justifications for issuance of MD that supervisors can utilize. Use of the SOP will result in both more efficient methods of acquiring MD accessories (through eBusiness) while providing information about their necessity and likely use.

e. Include standard procedures for addressing inappropriate use of a MD, including consequences.

Concur. The planned SOP will reference the Agency's conduct and discipline Order and the Agency's Disciplinary Handbook to determine appropriate consequences when inappropriate use of a MD is determined.

f. Develop eBusiness design changes that would trigger the system to notify account managers when a predetermined cost threshold is reached, which may indicate potentially inappropriate use of a MD.

Do not concur. OEI believes there are adequate information sources currently available for individual account managers to monitor mobile device usage without the establishment of thresholds. OEI/OTOP will continue to work with account managers to educate them on usage reports.

In December 2011, this request was put before the eBusiness Configuration Control Board (CCB) under request number 11871, and it was disapproved as an ineffective approach to managing usage under the pooled minutes plan. The Board noted that the eBusiness sorting capability will support reviewing bills from high to low values to review charges in lieu of maintaining thresholds. This Board is primarily made up of customer representatives from the different EPA program and regional offices.

eBusiness currently offers a service specific report for all mobile devices which displays account information, office, user, charges, minutes used, rate plan and device. The report can be sorted to review minutes used by account by user without the need to set thresholds. Since the Mobile Device Service has moved from individual rate plans to Agency-wide pooled minutes, no one is assigned to a measureable rate plan. A threshold would have to be set for each user based on an average of "normal" device activity. Since the inception of the pooled minutes plan, the EPA has not exceeded the total pool threshold and no additional charges for additional minutes have occurred. In addition, we currently have an EPA inventory of just under 6,600 units which would make the individual calculation of thresholds an unnecessary expense.

g. Allow approved users to possess either a cell phone or a BlackBerry, or require additional documented justification and annual review if an employee requires multiple devices.

Concur. OPRO will include within the planned SOP a standardized business case justification for MD issuance. This information can assist supervisors in determining if additional devices are needed.

h. Review the business need for MD users with low utilization of their monthly plan minute allotments (less than I, 10, 20, and 30 percent utilization as described in EPA's Mobile Device Service Review and Optimization Analysis) and terminate service where appropriate.

Concur. OPRO will include in the planned SOP a quarterly review of zero usage reports from the cell carriers and termination of service where appropriate. Utilization of plan minutes is not the best indicator of device use, as a review of Service reports indicates that many users with high use of their device primarily use the data functions of the MD for text and email, while using only a minimal number of voice minutes.

i.   Require end users to notify their property staff when they no longer need a device, transfer to another EPA program office, or leave the Agency. Instruct end users on the proper procedure for turning in their MDs.

Concur. OPRO will include within the planned SOP for employee provisioning/deprovisioning a step that the employee notifies property staff if they no longer need a device. In addition, OPRO will ensure that the SOP for the custodial officer and WCF account manager includes coordination of a quarterly review of employee devices and usage.

2.   Follow up with OEI managers and determine:

a.   Whether there is a valid business case justification for those staff using multiple MDs, and determine whether one of the devices should be returned to the Agency.

Concur. The planned SOP will develop standardized business case justifications for issuing a MD that supervisors can utilize. In cases where multiple devices have been issued, OEI will develop the SOP to require supervisors to review justifications annually by coordinating with the WCF account manager.

b.   Whether the international calls made during January-June 2011 by the remaining 19 OEI employees and contractors we identified in our sample of 27 were inappropriate, and take action based on SOPs developed per recommendation 1.

Concur. OEI plans to follow up with managers and determine if the identified employees fall within the Agency's conduct and discipline Order and the Agency's Disciplinary Handbook. For contractors that have been identified, OEI management will request the Contracting Officer and Contracting Officer Representative investigate the use of the MD and will take appropriate steps as allowed under the contract.

3.   Finalize Agency-wide draft domestic and international MD procedures and develop other Agency-wide procedures as necessary that consider SOPs that encompass the areas listed in recommendation 1.

Concur.
OEI believes that two actions should be created for this recommendation.
   1.   Finalize the procedure for domestic use which OEI OTOP leads.
   2.   Finalize the procedure for international use which the OEI SAISO leads.

OTOP Corrective Action: Finalize the draft Mobile Device and Wireless Procedure by the end of calendar year 2012.

SAISO Corrective Action: A procedure addressing international travel for mobile devices has been drafted and we expect to have a final version by October 1, 2012.

Should you have any questions regarding our corrective action plan, please contact Scott Dockum at 202-566-1914 or dockum.scott@epa.gov.

cc: Rudolph Brevard, Office of Inspector General, OMS
Pat Hill, Office of Inspector General, OMS
James McDonald, Office of Environmental Information, OPRO
Robert McKinney, Office of Environmental Information, SAISO
Vaughn Noga, Office of Environmental Information, OTOP
Scott Dockum, Office of Environmental Information, OPRO

Distribution

Office of the Administrator
Assistant Administrator for Environmental Information and Chief Information Officer
Agency Follow-Up Official (the CFO)
Agency Follow-Up Coordinator
General Counsel
Associate Administrator for Congressional and Intergovernmental Relations
Associate Administrator for External Affairs and Environmental Education
Audit Follow-Up Coordinator, Office of Environmental Information

www.ingramcontent.com/pod-product-compliance
Lightning Source LLC
Chambersburg PA
CBHW081330310526
45789CB00018B/3080

* 9 7 8 1 5 0 0 5 6 3 0 7 3 *